March of America Facsimile Series

Number 22

A Relation of Maryland

A Relation of Maryland

ANN ARBOR

UNIVERSITY MICROFILMS, INC.

A Subsidiary of Xerox Corporation

Foreword

A Relation of Maryland, 1635, was printed to attract adventurers to settle in the newly-founded Province of Maryland. It is one of the most elaborate of the promotion tracts written in behalf of an American colony.

In 1632 Charles I granted a charter to Cecil Calvert, second baron Baltimore, making him the proprietor of the largest tract of land granted to a single person up to that time. Lord Baltimore's father, George Calvert, first baron Baltimore, had been the promoter of the charter. He had previously received a land grant in Newfoundland but found the climate there unsuitable for colonization. Before returning to England he had sailed up the Chesapeake Bay and, finding Maryland more to his liking than Newfoundland, petitioned the King for a grant to that land. George Calvert died shortly before the issue of a charter, but his son Cecil succeeded him to his title and to the land.

In November, 1633, two ships, *The Ark* and *The Dove*, set sail for the New World with both Catholics and Protestants aboard. Lord Baltimore, a Catholic, hoped to find in Maryland a place of refuge for his Catholic brethren, who were unwelcome in the colonies of Virginia and New England. Since Baltimore needed settlers to make his colony survive, he readily accepted those of any faith who were willing to come. Baltimore introduced a policy of religious toleration, but his efforts were sometimes frustrated. The colony was a success, but when the Puritans gained control of the government they rescinded Baltimore's act of toleration.

An account of the first year in Maryland, written by one of the early settlers, thought to be the Jesuit priest, Father Andrew White, was entitled *A Relation of the successful beginnings of the Lord Baltimore's plantation in Maryland* (1634). The first chapter of the present 1635 *Relation* is an abridgement of Father White's narrative. It recounts the voyage, the meeting with the Indians, and the settlement at St. Mary's. The remaining chapters tell of the advantages of settling in Maryland, the "conditions propounded by Lord Baltimore," and the provisions necessary for each settler. The list of provisions and equipment comes almost word for word from John Smith's *Generall Historie of Virginia*. Appended to the *Relation* is a map of Maryland and the Charter translated from Latin into English. This charter was granted by a Protestant king to a Catholic subject without qualifications. It conferred on Lord Baltimore the authority of a count palatine, making him virtually a king within his own province. He had the power to make and publish the laws of the land, with the stipulation, however, that they be with the "advise, assent, and approbation of the free-men." Although Lord Baltimore in fact had the powers of a feudal lord, the old medieval system was not to the liking of the free men of Maryland, who put their own interpretation on "advise, assent, and approbation." The second assembly which met in 1639 rejected the code of laws sent over by the Proprietor and drew up its own ordinance to which Lord Baltimore had to agree.

This work is discussed by Lawrence C. Wroth in an article "The Maryland Colonization Tracts, 1632-1646," which was published in *Essays Offered to Herbert Putnam* (New Haven, 1929) pp. 539-555.

A Relation of Maryland

A

RELATION

OF

MARYLAND;

Together,

VVith {
A Map of the Countrey,
The Conditions of Plantation,
His Majesties Charter to the
Lord *Baltemore*, translated
into English.

These Bookes are to bee had, at Master *William Peasley* Esq; his house, on the back-side of *Drury-Lane*, neere the *Cock-pit* Playhouse; or in his absence, at Master *Iohn Morgans* house in high *Holbourne*, over against the *Dolphin*,
London.

September the 8. *Anno Dom.* 1635.

Chap. I.

A RELATION
Of the Lord BALTEMORE'S
Plantation in *Maryland*.

Is most Excellent Majestie
Having by His Letters Pa-
tents, under the Great
Seale of *England*, granted a
certaine Countrey in *America* (now called *Maryland*,
in honour of our gratious
Queene) unto the Lord *Bal-
temore*, with divers Priviledges, and encouragements to all those that should adventure
with his Lordship in the planting of that Cōn-
trey: the benefit and honour of such an action
was readily apprehended by divers Gentlemen,
of good birth and qualitie, who thereupon resolued to adventure their persons, and a good
A 2   part

part of their fortunes with his Lordſhip, in the
purſuite of ſo noble and (in all likelihood)
ſo aduantagious an enterprize. His Lordſhip
was at firſt reſolued to goe in perſon; but the
more important reaſons perſwading his ſtay at
home, hee appointed his brother, Mr. *Leonard
Caluert* to goe Governour in his ſtead, with
whom he joyned in Commiſſion, Mr. *Ierome
Hawley*, and Mr. *Thomas Cornwallis*(two worthy
and able Gentlemen.) Theſe with the other
Gentlemen aduenturers, and their ſeruants, to
the number of neere 200. people, imbarked
theſelues for the voyage, in the good ſhip called
the *Arke*, of 300. tunne & upward, which was
attended by his Lordſhips Pinnace, called the
Dove, of about 50. tunne. And ſo on Friday,
the 22. of *November*, 1633. a ſmall gale of
winde comming gently from the *North-
weſt*, they weighed from the *Cowes* in the *Iſle*
of *Wight*, about ten in the morning; And
having ſtayed by the way Twenty dayes at
the *Barbada's*, and Fourteene dayes at Saint
Chriſtophers (upon ſome neceſſary occaſions)
they arrived at *Point Comfort* in *Virginia*, on the
foure & twentyeth of *February* following. They
had Letters from his Majeſty, in favor of them,
to the Governour of *Virginia*; in obedience
whereunto, he uſed them with much courteſie
and humanitie. At this time, one Captaine
Cleyborne(one of the Councel of *Virginia*)com-
ming

ming from the parts whether they intended to goe, told them that all the Natives were in preparation of defence by reason of a rumor some had raised amongst them, that 6. shippes were to come with many people, who would drive all the inhabitants out of the Countrey.

On the 3. of *March*, they left *Point-Comfort*, & 2. dayes after, they came to *Patowmeck* river, which is about 24. leagues distant, there they began to give names to places, and called the *Southerne* point of that River, Saint *Gregories*; and the *Northerne* point, Saint *Michaels*, *Patowmeck*, is a great *River of the Province of Maryland: on which they intended, to seate the first Colony.*

They sayled up the River, till they came to *Heron* Iland, which is about 14. leagues, and there came to an Anchor under an Island neere unto it, which they called S. *Clements*. Where they set up a Crosse, and tooke possession of this Countrey for our *Saviour*, and for our Soveraigne Lord the King of *England*. *So called from the aboundance of that Fowle there.*

Heere the Governor thought fit for the ship to stay, vntill hee had discovered more of the Countrey: and so hee tooke two Pinnaces, and went up the River some 4. leagues, and landed on the *South* side, where he found the *Indians* fled for feare, from thence hee sayled some 9. leagues higher to *Patowmeck* Towne, where the *Werowance* being a child, *Archihau* his vnckle (who governed him and his Countrey for him) gave all the company good wellcome, and one of the company having entered into a little dis- *The Dove, and one hyred in Virginia.* *So they call their Princes.*

coarse

courſe with him , touching the errours of
their religion, hee ſeemed well pleaſed there-
with; and at his going away , deſired him to returne thither againe, ſaying he ſhould live with
him, his men ſhould hunt for him , and hee
would divide all with him.

From hence the Governor went to *Paſchatoway*,
about 20. leagues higher, where he found many
Indians aſſembled, and heere he met with one
Captaine *Henry Fleete* an *Engliſh-man*, who had
lived many yeeres among the *Indians*, and by
that meanes ſpake the Countrey language very
well, and was much eſteemed of by the natives.
Him our Governour ſent a ſhore to invite the
werowance to a parley , who thereupon came
with him aboard privatly, where he was courte-
ouſly entertained , and after ſome parley being
demanded by the Governour, whether hee
would be content that he and his people ſhould
ſet downe in his Countrey , in caſe he ſhould
find a place conuenient for him , his anſwere
was, "*that he would not bid him goe ,neither would*
"*hee bid him ſtay, but that he might uſe his owne*
"*diſcretion.*

While this *werowance* was aboard, many of
his people came to the water ſide , fearing that
he might be ſurpriſed , whereupon the *wero-*
rance commanded two *Indians* that came with
him, to goe on ſhore, to quit them of this feare,
but they anſwered , they feared they would kill
them ;

them; The *werowance* therefore shewed himselfe upon the decke, and told them hee was in
safety, wherewith they were satisfied.

Whilest the Governour was abroad, the
neighbouring *Indians*, where the ship lay, began to cast off feare, and to come to their
Court of guard, which they kept night and day
upon Saint *Clements* Ile, partly to defend their
barge, which was brought in pieces out of *England*, and there made up; and partly to defend
their men which were imployed in felling of
trees, and cleaving pales for a Palizado, and at
last they ventured to come aboard the ship.

The Governour finding it not fit, for many
reasons, to seate himselfe as yet so high in the
River, resolued to returne backe againe, and to
take a more exact view of the lower parts, and
so leaving the Ship & Pinnaces there, he tooke
his Barge(as most fit to search the Creekes,
and small rivers) and was conducted by Captaine *Fleete* (who knew well the Countrey) to
a River on the North-side of *Patomeck* river,
within 4. or 5. leagues from the mouth thereof,
which they called Saint *Georges* River. They
went up this river about 4. Leagues, and an-
chored at the Towne of *Yoacomaco* : from
whence the *Indians* of that part of the Countrey, are called the *Yoacomacoes* :

~At their comming to this place, the Governour went on shoare, and treated friendly
B   with

with the *weromance* there, and acquainted him
with the intent of his comming thither, to
which hee made little anſwere (as it is their
manner, to any new or ſuddaine queſtion) but
entertained him, and his company that night in
his houſe, and gave him his owne bed to lie on
(which is a matt layd on boords) and the next
day, went to ſhew him the country; and that day
being ſpent in viewing the places about that
towne, and the freſh waters, which there are very plentifull, and excellent good (but the
maine rivers are ſalt) the Governor determined
to make the firſt Colony there, and ſo gave order for the Ship and Pinnaces to come thither.

This place he found to be a very commodious ſituation for a Towne, in regard the land is
good, the ayre wholſome and pleaſant, the River affords a ſafe harbour for ſhips of any bur-
then, and a very bould ſhoare ; freſh water, and
wood there is in great plenty, and the place ſo
naturally fortified, as with little difficultie, it
will be defended from any enemie.

To make his entry peaceable. and ſafe, hee
thought fit to preſent the *weromance* and the
wiſoes of the Towne with ſome *Engliſh* Cloth,
(ſuch as is uſed in trade with the *Indians*) Axes, Howes, and Knives, which they accepted
very kindly, and freely gave conſent that hee
and his company ſhould dwell in one part of
their Towne, and reſerued the other for themſelues,

So they call
the chiefe
men of Ac-
compt a-
mongſt them.

felues : and thofe *Indians* that dwelt in that part of the Towne, which was allotted for the *Englifh*, freely left them their houfes, and fome corne that they had begun to plant: It was alfo agreed betweene them, that at the end of harueft they fhould leave the whole towne; which they did accordingly: And they made mutuall promifes to each other, to live friendly and peaceably together, and if any injury fhould happen to be done on any part, that fatisfaction fhould be made for the fame; and thus upon the 27. day of *March*, *Anno Domini*, 1634. the Governour tooke poffeffion of the place, and named the Towne Saint *Maries*.

There was an occafion that much facilitated their treaty with thefe *Indians*, which was this: The *Safquehanocks* (a warlike people that inhabite betweene *Chefopeack* bay, and *Delaware* bay) did vfually make warres, and incurfions upon the neighbouring *Indians*, partly for fuperiority, partly for to get their Women, and what other purchafe they could meet with, which thefe *Indians* of *Yacomaco* fearing, had the yeere before our arivall there, made a refolution, for their fafety, to remove themfelues higher into the Countrey where it was more populous, and many of them were gone thither before the *Englifh* arrived.

Three dayes after their comming to *Yacomaco* the Arke with the two Pinaces arived there:

The

The *Indians* much wondred to see such ships, and at the thundering of the Ordnance when they came to an Anchor.

The next day they began to prepare for their houses, and first of all a Court of Guard, and a Store-house; in the meane time they lay a-bord the ship: They had not beene there many dayes before *Sir Iohn Haruie* the governor of *Virginea* came thither to visit them; Also some Indian *Werowances*; and many other Indians from severall parts came to see them, amongst others the *Werowance* of *Patuxent* came to visit the Governour, and being brought into the great Cabin of the ship, was placed betweene the Governour of *Virginea*, and the Governour of *Mary-land*; and a *Patuxent* Indian that came with him, comming into the Cabin, and finding the *Werowance* thus sitting betweene the two Governours, started backe, fearing the *Werowance* was surprised; and was ready to have leapt overboard, and could not be perswaded to come into the Cabin, untill the *Werowance* came himselfe unto him; for he remembred how the said *Werowance* had formerly beene taken prisoner by the *English* of *Virginia*.

After they had finished the store-house, and unladed the ship, the Governour thought fit to bring the Colours on shore, which were attended by all the Gentlemen, and the rest of the servants in armes; who received the Colours with

with a volley of fhot, which was anfwered by the Ordnance from the fhips; At this Ceremony were prefent, the *Werowances* of *Patuxent*, and *Yoacomaco*, with many other Indians; and the *Werowance* of *Patuxent* hereupon tooke occafion to advife the Indians of *Yoacomaco* to be carefull to keepe the league that they had made with the *Englifh*. He ftayed with them divers dayes, and ufed many Indian Complements, and at his departure hee faid to the Governour. "I loue the *Englifh* fo well, that if "they fhould goe about to kill me, if I had but "fo much breath as to fpeake; I would com-"mand the people, not to revenge my death; "for I know they would not doe fuch a thing, "except it were through mine owne default.

They brought thither with them fome ftore of Indian Corne, from the *Barbado's*, which at their firft arivall they began to vfe (thinking fit to referve their Englifh provifion of Meale and Oatemeale) and the Indian women feeing their fervants to bee unacquainted with the manner of dreffing it, would make bread thereof for them; and teach them how to doe the like: They found alfo the countrey well ftored with Corne (which they bought with truck, fuch as there is defired, the Natiues having no knowledge of the ufe of money) whereof they fold them fuch plenty, as that they fent 1000. bufhells of it to *New-England*, to provide them

fome

some salt-fish, and other commodities which they wanted.

During the time that the *Indians* stai'd by the English at *Yoacomaco*, they went dayly to hunt with them for Deere and Turkies,wherof some they gaue them for Presents, and the meaner sort would sell them to them,for knives,beades and the like : Also of Fish,the natives brought them great store, and in all things dealt very friendly with them ; their women and children came very frequently amongst them,which was a certaine signe of their confidence of them, it being found by experience, that they never attempt any ill,where the women are, or may be in danger.

Their comming thus to seate upon an Indian Towne, where they found ground cleered to their hands, gave them opportunity (although they came late in the yeere) to plant some Corne,and to make them gardens,which they sowed with English seeds of all sorts, and they prospered exceeding well. They also made what haste they could to finish their houses ; but before they could accomplish all these things,one Captaine *Cleyborne* (who had a desire to appropriate the trade of those parts unto himselfe)began to cast out words amongst the Indians, saying, That those of *Yoacomaco* were *Spaniards* and his enemies ; and by this meanes endeavoured to alienate the mindes of the

the Natives from them, so that they did not receive them so friendly as formerly they had done. This caused them to lay aside all other workes, and to finish their Fort, which they did within the space of one moneth; where they mounted some Ordnance, and furnished it with some murtherers, and such other meanes of defence as they thought fit for their safeties: which being done, they proceeded with their Houses and finished them, with convenient accommodations belonging thereto: And although they had thus put themselves in safety, yet they ceased not to procure to put these jealousies out of the Natives minds, by treating and vsing them in the most courteous manner they could, and at last prevailed therein, and setled a very firme peace and friendship with them. They procured from *Virginia*, Hogges, Poultrey, and some Cowes, and some male cattell, which hath given them a foundation for breed and increase; and whoso desires it, may furnish himselfe with store of Cattell from thence, but the hogges and Poultrey are already increased in *Maryland*, to a great stocke, sufficient to serve the Colonie very plentifully. They have also set up a Water-mill for the grinding of Corne, adjoyning to the Towne.

Thus within the space of sixe moneths, was laid the foundation of the Colonie in *Maryland*; and whosoever intends now to goe thither

ther, shall finde the way so troden, that hee may proceed with much more ease and confidence then these first adventurers could, who were ignorant both of Place, People, and all things else, and could expect to find nothing but what nature produced : besides, they could not in reason but thinke, the Natives would oppose them ; whereas now the Countrey is discovered, and friendship with the Natives is assured, houses built, and many other accommodations, as Cattell, Hogges, Poultry, Fruits and the like brought thither from *England*, *Virginea*, and other places, which are vsefull, both for profit and Pleasure : and without boasting it may be said, that this Colony hath arived to more in sixe moneths, then *Virginia* did in as many yeeres. If any man say, they are beholding to *Virginea* for so speedy a supply of many of those things which they of *Virginia* were forced to fetch from *England* and other remote places, they will confesse it, and acknowledge themselves glad that *Virginea* is so neere a neighbour, and that it is so well stored of all necessaries for to make those parts happy, and the people to live as plentifully as in any other part of the world, only they wish that they would be content their neighbours might live in peace by them, and then no doubt they should find a great comfort each in other:

CHAP.

Chap. II.

A description of the Countrey.

THe precedent difcourfe gives you to underftand, how the firft Colony fate downe in *Maryland*, what progreffe they made, and in what eftate it is at this prefent: Now my purpofe is to fpeake of the Countrey in generall, that who fo lookes that way, may beforehand know fomething thereof. It is feated betweene the degrees of 38 and 40 of North-Latitude, *Virginia* bounds it on the South, *New-England* on the North, and the Ocean on the Eaft, but the Wefterne parts are not yet difcovered.

The temper of the Ayre is very good, and agrees well with the Englifh, as appeared at their firft comming thither, when they had no houfes to fhelter them, and their people were

C   enforced

enforced, not onely to labour in the day, but to watch in their turnes at night, yet had their healths exceeding well : In Summer its hot as in *Spaine*, and in Winter there is frost and snow, but it seldome lasts long ; this last Winter was the coldest that had beene knowne in many yeeres : but the yeere before, there was scarce any signe of Winter, onely that the leaves fell from the trees, in all other things it appeared to be Summer; and yet the last Winter, both their Cattell and Hoggs kept themselves in the woods, without any fodder, or other helpe, and the Hoggs thrived so well, that some of them were killed out of the woods for Porke and Bacon, which was excellent good and fat.

The Windes there are variable; from the South comes Heat, Gusts, and Thunder; from the North, or North-west, cold-weather, and in winter, Frost and Snow; from the East and South-east, Raine.

The ordinary entrance by Sea into this Countrey, is betweene two Capes, which are distant each from other, about 7 or 8 leagves, the South-Cape is called *Cape-Henry*; the North, *Cape-Charles*, When you are come within the *Capes*, you enter into a faire Bay, which is navigable for at least 200 miles, and is called *Chesopeack* Bay, and runneth Northerly : Into this Bay fall many goodly navigable

Rivers,

Rivers, the chiefe whereof is *Patomack*, where the Colony is now feated. It's navigable for 140 miles, it begins to be fresh about 2 leagues above *Patomack* Towne. The next River North-ward is *Patuxent*, which at the entrance is di-stant from the other, about 20 miles, and is a very pleafant and commodious River; It's fit for habitation, and eafie to be defended, by rea-fon of the Ilands, and other places of advantage, that may command it; from thence, untill you come to the head of the Bay, there are no more Rivers that are inhabited : There dwell the *Saf-quehanocks*, upon a River that is not navigable for our Boates, by reafon of Sholes and Rockes; but they paffe it in * *Canoos* ; At the entrance thereof, there is an Iland which will command that River. Vpon the Eaft fide of this Bay lie very many Ilands which are not inhabited, where are ftore of Deere.

*A tearme they ufe for their Boates.

On the Eafterne fhore of the Country, which lieth upon the maine Ocean, are fundry fmall Creekes, and one likely to proove a very com-modious harbour, called *Matfopongue*; neere the mouth whereof, lieth an Iland of about 20 miles in length, and thence about 6 leagues more Northerly, another Iland called *Chingoto*; and about feaven leagues beyond that, to the North, opens another very large faire Bay, cal-led *Delaware* Bay. This Bay is about 8 leagues wide at the entrance, and into it, there falls a

C 2
very

very faire navigable River.

The Countrey is generally plaine and even, and yet hath some pritty small hills and risings; It's full of Rivers and Creekes, and hath store of Springs and small Brookes: The Woods for the most part are free from underwood, so that a man may travell on horsebacke, almost any-where, or hunt for his recreation.

CHAP.

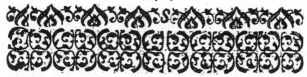

Chap. III.

The Commodities which this Countrey affords naturally.

THis Countrey affords naturally, many excellent things for Physicke and Surgery, the perfect use of which, the *English* cannot yet learne from the Natives: They have a roote which is an excellent preseruative against Poyson, called by the *English*, the *Snake roote*. Other herbes and rootes they have, wherewith they cure all manner of woundes; also *Saxafras*, Gummes, and *Balsum*. An *Indian* seeing one of the *English*, much troubled with the tooth-ake, fetched of the roote of a tree, and gave the party some of it to hold in his mouth, and it eased the paine presently. They have other rootes fit for dyes, wherewith they make colours to paint themselues.

The

The Timber of thefe parts is very good, and in aboundance, it is ufefull for building of houfes, and fhippes; the white Oake is good for Pipe-ftaves, the red Oake for wainefcot. There is alfo Walnut, Cedar, Pine, & Cipreffe, Chefnut, Elme, Afhe, and Popler, all which are for Building, and Husbandry. Alfo there are divers forts of Fruit-trees, as Mulberries, Perfimons, with feverall other kind of Plummes, and Vines, in great aboundance. The Maft and the Chefnuts, and what rootes they find in the woods, doe feede the Swine very fat, and will breede great ftore, both for their owne provifion, or for merchandife, and fuch as is not inferior to the Bacon of *weftphalia*.

Of Strawberries, there is plenty, which are ripe in *Aprill*: Mulberries in *May*; and Rafpices in *Iune*; Maracocks which is fomewhat like a Limon, are ripe in *Auguft*.

In the Spring, there are feverall forts of herbes, as Corn-fallet, Violets, Sorrell, Purflaine, all which are very good and wholfome, and by the *English*, ufed for fallets, and in broth.

In the upper parts of the Countrey, there are Bufeloes, Elkes, Lions, Beares, Wolues, and Deare there are great ftore, in all places that are not too much frequented, as alfo Beavers, Foxes, Otters, and many other forts of Beafts.

Of Birds, there is the Eagle, Gofhawke, Falcon, Lanner, Sparrow-hawke, and Merlin,

alſo wild Turkeys in great aboundance, whereof many weigh 50. pounds, and upwards; and of
Partridge plenty : There are likewiſe ſundry
ſorts of Birds which ſing, whereof ſome are red,
ſome blew, others blacke and yellow, ſome like
our Black-birds, others like Thruſhes, but not
of the ſame kind, with many more, for which
wee know no names.

In Winter there is great plenty of Swannes,
Cranes, Geeſe, Herons, Ducke, Teale, Widge-
on, Brants, and Pidgeons, with other ſorts,
whereof there are none in *England*.

The Sea, the Bayes of *Cheſopeack*, and *Delaware*, and generally all the Rivers, doe abound
with Fiſh of ſeverall ſorts; for many of them wo
have no *Engliſh* names : There are Whales,
Sturgeons uery large and good, and in great a-
boundance; Grampuſes, Porpuſes, Mullets,
Trouts, Soules, Place, Mackerell, Perch, Crabs,
Oyſters, Cockles, and Muſsles; But above all
theſe, the fiſh that have no Engliſh names, are
the beſt except the Sturgeons : There is alſo a
fiſh like the Thornebacke in *England*, which
hath a taile a yard long, wherein are ſharpe
prickles, with which if it ſtrike a man, it will
put him to much paine and torment, but it is
very good meate : alſo the Tode-fiſh, which
will ſwell till it be ready to burſt, if it be taken
out of the water.

The Mineralls have not yet beene much
ſearched

ARIÆ tabula

Portobacke.
Peynt.
Pascatoway.
Matapanian.
ent.
CK   bay
Moneponson
Wicamate

Sasquehannocks.   N O V Æ

Delaware Bay

A N G L I Æ

P A R S

T. Cecill sculp:

HONI SOIT QVI MALY PENSE
DIEV ET MON DROIT

Fatti   Maschij: Parole   Femine

40   41

298
299
300
301
302

searched after, yet there is discovered Iron Oare and Earth fitt to make Allum, *Terra lemnia*, and a red soile like Bolearmonicke; with sundry other sorts of Mineralls, which wee have not yet beene able to make any tryall of.

The soile generally is very rich, like that which is about *Cheesweeke* neere *London*, where it is worth 20.shillings an Acre yeerely to Tillage in the Common-fields, and in very many places, you shall have two foote of blacke rich mould, wherein you shall scarce find a stone, it is like a sifted Garden-mould, and is so rich, that if it be not first planted with *Indian* corne, *Tobacco*, Hempe, or some such thing that may take off the ranknesse thereof, it will not be fit for any *English* graine; and under that, there is found good loame, whereof wee have made as good bricke as any in *England*; there is great store of Marish ground also, that with good husbandry, will make as rich Medow, as any in the world : There is store of Marle, both blue, and white, and in many places, excellent clay for pots, and tyles; and to conclude, there is nothing that can be reasonably expected in a place lying in the latitude which this doth, but you shall either find it here to grow naturally, or Industry, and good husbandry will produce it.

C H A P.

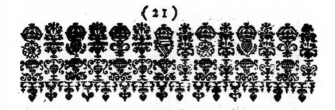

Chap. IIII.

The commodities that may be procured in *Maryland* by industry.

Ee that well confiders the fitua-
tion of this Countrey, and findes
it placed betweene *Virginia* and
New-England, cannot but, by his
owne reafon, conclude that it
muft needs participate of the naturall commodities of both places, and be capable of thofe
which induftry brings into either, the diftan-
ces being fo fmall betweene them : you fhall
find in the Southerne parts of *Maryland,* all
that *Virginia* hath naturally ; and in the Northerne parts, what *New-England* produceth; and
he that reades Captaine *Iohn Smith* fhall fee at
large difcourfed what is in *Virginia,* and in Mafter *William Wood,* who this yeere hath written a

D   trea-

treatife of *New-England*, he may know what is there to be expected.

Yet to say something of it in particular.

IN the firft place I name Corne, as the thing moft neceffary to fuftaine man; That which the Natives ufe in the Countrey, makes very good bread, and alfo a meate which they call *Omene*, it's like our *Furmety*, and is very favory and wholefome; it will Mault and make good Beere; Alfo the Natives have a fort of *Pulfe*, which we call *Peafe* and *Beanes*, that are very good. This Corne yeelds a great increafe, fo doth the *Peafe* and *Beanes* : One man may in a feafon, well plant fo much as will yeeld a hundred bufhells of this Corne, 20 bufhells of *Beanes* and *Peafe*, and yet attend a crop of *Tobacco* : which according to the goodneffe of the ground may be more or leffe, but is ordinarily accompted betweene 800 and 1000 pound weight.

They have made tryall of Englifh *Peafe*, and they grow very well, alfo *Musk-mellons*, *Watermellons*, *Cow-cumbers*, with all forts of garden Roots and Herbes, as *Carrots*, *Parfenips*, *Turnips*, *Cabbages* R:difh with many more; and in *Virginia* they have fowed Englifh *wheate* and *Barley*, and it yeelds twife as much increafe as in *England*; and although there be not many that doe apply themfelves to plant Gardens and Orchards, yet thofe that doe it, find much pro-

fit

fit and pleasure thereby: They have Peares, Apples, and severall sorts of Plummes, Peaches in abundance, and as good as those of *Italy*; so are the Mellons and Pumpions: Apricocks, Figgs and Pomegranates prosper exceedingly; they haue lately planted Orange and Limon trees which thrive very wel: and in fine, there is scarce any fruit that growes in *England, France, Spaine,* or *Italy,* but hath been tryed there, and prospers well. You may there also have Hemp and Flax, Pitch and Tarre, with little labour; it's apt for Rapeseed, and Annis-seed, Woad, Madder, Saffron, &c. There may be had, Silke-wormes, the Countrey being stored with Mulberries: and the superfluity of wood will produce Potashes.

And for *wine*, there is no doubt but it will be made there in plenty, for the ground doth naturally bring foorth Vines, in such aboundance, that they are as frequent there, as Brambles are here. *Iron* may be made there with little charge; Brave ships may be built, without requiring any materialls from other parts: Clabboard, Wainscott, Pipestaves and Masts for ships the woods will afford plentifully. In fine, *Butter* and *Cheese, Porke* and *Bacon,* to transport to other countrys will be no small commodity, which by industry may be quickly had there in great plenty, &c. And if there were no other staple commodities to be hoped for, but Silke and Linnen (the materialls of which, apparantly will grow there) it were sufficient to enrich the inhabitants.   D 2   C H A P.

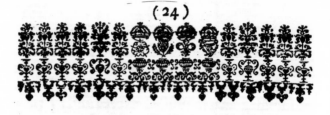

Chap. V.

Of the Naturall disposition of the *Indians* which Inhabite the parts of *Maryland* where the *English* are seated : And their manner of living.

HEE that hath a Curiosity to know all that hath beene obserued of the Customes and manners of the *Indians*, may find large discourses thereof in Captaine *Smiths* Booke of *Virginia*, and Mr. *Woods* of *New-England* : but he that is desirous to goe to *Maryland*, shall heere find enough to informe him of what is necessary for him to know touching them.

By

By Captaine *Smith's*, and many other Relations you may be informed, that the People are War-licke, and have done much harme to the *English*; and thereby are made very terrible. Others say that they are a base and cowardly People, and to be contemned: and it is thought by some who would be esteemed Statef-men, that the only point of pollicie that the *English* can use, is, to destroy the *Indians*, or to drive them out of the Countrey, without which, it is not to be hoped that they can be secure. The truth is, if they be injured, they may well be feared, they being People that have able bodies, and generally, taller, and bigger limbed then the *English*, and want not courage; but the oddes wee have of them in our weapons, keepes them in awe, otherwise they would not flie from the *English*, as they have done in the time of Warres with those of *Virginia*, and out of that respect, a small number of our men being armed, will adventure upon a great troope of theirs, and for no other reason, for they are resolute and subtile enough: But from hence to conclude, that there can be no safety to live with them, is a very great errour. Experience hath taught us, that by kind and faire usage, the Natives are not onely become peaceable, but also friendly, and have upon all occasions performed as many friendly Offices to the *English* in *Maryland*, and *New-England*, as any neighbour

bour

bour or friend uses to doe in the most Civill parts of Christendome : Therefore any wise man will hold it a far more just and reasonable way to treat the People of the Countrey well, thereby to induce them to civility, and to teach them the use of husbandry, and Mechanick trades, whereof they are capable, which may in time be very usefull to the *English*; and the Planters to keepe themselues strong, and united in Townes, at least for a competent number, and then noe man can reasonably doubt, either surprise, or any other ill dealing from them.

But to proceede, hee that sees them, may know how men lived whilest the world was under the Law of Nature; and as by nature, so amongst them, all men are free, but yet subject to command for the publike defence. Their Government is Monarchicall, he that governes in chiefe, is called the *Werowance*, and is assisted by some that consult with him of the common affaires, who are called *Wisoes* : They have no Lawes, but the Law of Nature and discretion, by which all things are ruled, onely Custome hath introduced a law for the Succession of the Government, which is this; when a *werowance* dieth, his eldest sonne succeeds, and after him the second, and so the rest, each for their liues, and when all the sonnes are dead, then the sons of the *Werowances* eldest daughter shall succeede, and so if he have more daughters; for

they

they hold, that the issue of the daughters hath more of his blood in them than the issue of his sonnes. The *wisoes* are chosen at the pleasure of the *Werowance*, yet commonly they are chosen of the same family, if they be of yeeres capable: The yong men generally beare a very great respect to the elder.

They have also *Cockoroofes* that are their Captains in time of war, to whom they are very obedient; But the *weromance* himselfe plants Corne, makes his owne Bow and Arrowes, his Canoo, his Mantle, Shooes, and what ever else belongs unto him, as any other common Indian; and commonly the Commanders are the best and most ingenious and active in all those things which are in esteeme amongst them. The women serve their husbands, make their bread, dresse their meate, such as they kill in hunting, or get by fishing; and if they have more wives then one, as some of them have (but that is not generall) then the best beloved wife performes all the offices of the house, and they take great content therein. The women also (beside the houshold businesse) use to make Matts, which serve to cover their houses, and for beds; also they make baskets, some of Rushes, others of Silke-grasse, which are very handsom.

The Children live with their Parents; the Boyes untill they come to the full growth of men; (for they reckon not by yeeres, as we doe)

then

then they are put into the number of Bow-men, and are called Blacke-boyes (and so continue untill they take them wives) When they are to be made Black-boyes, the ancient men that governe the yonger, tell them, That if they will be valiant and obedient to the *Weromance*, *wisos* and *Cokcorooses*, then their god will love them, all men will esteeme of them, and they shall kill Deere, and Turkies, catch Fish, and all things shall goe well with them; but if otherwise, then shall all goe contrary: which perswasion mooves in them an incredible obedience to their commands; If they bid them take fire in their hands or mouthes, they will doe it, or any other desperate thing, although with the apparant danger of their lives.

The women remaine with their Parents untill they have husbands, and if the Parents bee dead, then with some other of their friends. If the husband die, he leaves all that he hath to his wife, except his bow and arrowes, and some Beades (which they usually bury with them) and she is to keepe the children untill the sons come to be men, and then they live where they please, for all mens houses are free unto them; and the daughters untill they have husbands. The manner of their marriages is thus; he that would have a wife, treates with the father, or if he be dead, with the friend that takes care of her whom he desires to have to wife, and agrees with

with him for a quantity of Beades, or some such other thing which is accepted amongst them; which he is to give for her, and must be payed at the day of their marriage; and then the day being appointed, all the friends of both parts meet at the mans house that is to have the wife, and each one brings a present of meate and the woman that is to be married also brings her present: when the company is all come, the man he sits at the upper end of the house, and the womans friends leade her up, and place her by him, then all the company sit down upon mats, on the ground (as their manner is) and the woman riseth and serves dinner, First to her husband, then to all the company; the rest of the day they spend in singing and dancing (which is not unpleasant) at night the company leaves the, and comonly they live very peaceably and lovingly together; Yet it falls out sometimes, that a man puts away one wife and takes another; then she and her children returne to her friends again. They are generally very obedient to their husbands, and you shal seldome heare a woman speake in the presence of her husband, except he aske her some question.

This people live to a great age, which appeares, in that although they marry not so yong as we doe in *England*, yet you may see many of them great-grandfathers to children of good bignesse; and continue at that age, very

E   able

able and ſtrong men : The Men and Women
have all blacke haire,which is much bigger and
harſher then ours, it is rare to ſee any of them
to waxe gray, although they be very old , but
never bauld : It is ſeldome ſeene that any of the
men have beards , but they weare long locks,
which reach to their ſhoulders , and ſome of
them to their waſts : they are of a comely ſta-
ture, well favoured, and excellently well limbed , and ſeldome any deformed. In their
warres, and hunting , they uſe Bowes and Arrowes (but the Arrowes are not poyſoned, as in
other places.) The Arrow-heads are made of
a Flint-ſtone,the top of a Deares horne,or ſome
Fiſh-bone , which they faſten with a ſort of
glew, which they make. They alſo uſe in
warres , a ſhort club of a cubite long, which
they call a *Tomahawk.*

They live for the moſt part in Townes, like
Countrey Villages in *England*; Their houſes
are made like our Arboures, covered ſome
with matts , others with barke of trees , which
defend them from the injury of the weather:
The fiers are in the midſt of the houſe, and a
hole in the top for the ſmoake to goe out at.
In length,ſome of them are 30.others 40. ſome
a 100. foote; and in breadth about 12. foote.
They have ſome things amongſt them which
may well become Chriſtians to imitate, as
their temperance in eating and drinking, their

Iuſtice

Iuſtice each to other, for it is never heard of, that thoſe of a Nation will rob or ſteale one from another; and the *Engliſh* doe often truſt them with truck, to deale for them as factors, and they have performed it very juſtly: Alſo they have ſent letters by them to *Virginia*, and into other parts of the Countrey, unto their ſeruants that have beene trading abroad, and they have delivered them, and brought backe anſwere thereof unto thoſe that ſent them; Alſo their conuerſation each with other, is peaceable, and free from all ſcurrulous words, which may give offence; They are very hoſpitable to their owne people, and to ſtrangers; they are alſo of a grave comportment: Some of the Aduenturers at a time, was at one of their feaſts, when Two hundred of them did meet together; they eate of but one diſh at a meale, and every man, although there be never ſo many, is ſerued in a diſh by himſelfe; their diſhes are made of wood, but handſomely wrought: The dinner laſted two houres; and after dinner, they ſung and danced about two houres more, in all which time, not one word or action paſt amongſt them that could give the leaſt diſturbance to the company; In the moſt grave aſſembly, no man can expect to find ſo much time paſt with more ſilence and gravitie: Some *Indians* comming on a time to *Iames Towne* in *Virginia*, it happened, that there then ſate the Councell to heare

E 2   cauſes,

causes,and the *Indians* seeing such an assembly,
asked what it meant? Answere was made,there
was held a *Match-comaco* (which the *Indians*
call their place of Councell) the *Indian* replyed, that they all talke at once, but wee doe not
so in our *Match-comaco*.

Their attire is decent and modest ; about
their wasts, they weare a covering of Deares
skinnes, which reacheth to their knees, and upon their shoulders a large mantle of skinnes,
which comes downe to the middle of the
legge, and some to the heele ; in winter they
weare it furred, in summer without ; When
men hunt they put off their Mantles, so doe the
women when they worke,if the weather be hot :
The women affect to weare chaines and bracelets of beades, some of the better sort of them,
weare ropes of Pearle about their necks, and
some hanging in their eares,which are of a large
sort, but spoyled with burning the Oysters
in the fire, and the rude boaring of them. And
they and the young men use to paint their fa-
ces with severall colours, but since the *English*
came thither, those about them have quite left
it;and in many things shew a great inclination
to conforme themselues to the *English* manner
of living. The *werowance* of *Paschateway* desired the Governor to send him a man that could
build him a house like the English, and in sundry respects,commended our manner of living,

as

as much better then their owne: The *Werowance* of *Patuxent*, goes frequently in *English* Attire, so doth hee of *Portoback*, and many others that have bought Clothes of the *English* : These *Werowances* have made request, that some of their children may be brought up amongst the *English*, and every way, shew great demonstrations of friendship, and good affection unto them.

These People acknowledge a God, who is Their Religion. the giver of al the good things,wherewith their life is maintained ; and to him they sacrifice of the first fruits of their Corne,and of that which they get by hunting,and fishing : The sacrifice is performed by an Ancient man, who makes a speech unto their God (not without something of Barbarisme) which being ended, hee burnes part of the sacrifice., and then eates of the rest, then the People that are present, eate also, and untill the Ceremony be performed, they will not touch one bit thereof : They hold the Immortalitie of the soule , and that there is a place of Ioy, and another of torment after death, and that those which kill, steale, or lye, shall goe to the place of torment, but those which doe no harme, to the good place ; where they shall have all sorts of pleasure.

It happened the last yeere, that some of the *Sasquehanocks* and the *Wicomesses* (who are enemies) met at the Iland of *Monoponson*, where

E 3   Captaine

Captaine *Cleyborne* liveth, they all came to trade, and one of the *Sasquehanocks* did an Injury to a *Wicomesse*, whereat some of *Cleybornes* people that saw it, did laugh. The *Wicomesses* seeing themselues thus injured and despised (as they thought) went away, and lay in ambush for the returne of the *Sasquehanocks*, and killed five of them, onely two escaped; and then they returned againe, and killed three of *Cleybornes* People, and some of his Cattle; about two moneths after this was done, the *Wicomesses* sent a messenger unto his Lordships Governor, to excuse the fact, and to offer satisfaction for the harme that was done to the *English*: The *Wicomesse* that came with the message, brought in his company an *Indian*, of the Towne of *Patuxent*, which is the next neighbouring Towne unto the *English* at Saint *Maries*, with whom they have good correspondence, and hee spake to the Governour in this manner.

I Am a Native of *Patuxent*, as this man (whom you know) can tell you, true it is, I married a wife amongst the *Wicomesses*, where I have lived ever since, and they have sent me to tell you, that they are sorry for the harme, which was lately done by some of their people, to the *English* at *Monaponson*; and hope you will not make the rash act of a few young men, (which was done in heate) a quarrell to their Nation,

Nation, who defire to live in peace and love with you, and are ready to make fatisfaction for the Injury, defiring to know what will give you content, and that they will returne fuch things as were then taken from thence; But withall, they defire you not to thinke that they doe this for feare, for they have warres with the *Safquehanocks*, who have by a furprife, lately killed many of their men, but they would not fue to them for peace, intending to revenge the injuries, as they could find opportunitie, yet their defire was to have peace with the *English*.

The Governour returned anfwere to the *Wi-comeffe*; fince you acknowledge the Injury, and are forry for it, and onely defire to know what I expect for fatisfaction; I tell you I expect that thofe men, who have done this out-rage, fhould be delivered unto me, to doe with them as I fhall thinke fit, and likewife that you re-ftore all fuch things as you then tooke from the *English*; and withall, charged him with a fecond Injury attempted upon fome of his owne People, fince that time, by the *Wico-meffes*.

The *Wicomeffe* after a little paufe, replyed; It is the manner amongft us *Indians*, that if any fuch like accident happen, wee doe redeeme the life of a man that is fo flaine, with a 100. armes length of *Roanoke* (which is a fort of

Beades

Beades that they make, and use for money) and since that you are heere strangers, and come into our Countrey, you should rather conforme your selues to the Customes of our Countrey, then impose yours upon us ; But as for the second matter, I know nothing of it, nor can give any answere thereunto.

The Governour then told him ; It seemes you come not sufficiently instructed in the businesse which wee have with the *Wicomesses*, therefore tell them what I have said ; and that I expect a speedy answere ; and so dismist him.

It fell in the way of my discourse, to speake of the *Indian* money of those parts, It is of two sorts, *Wompompeag* and *Roanoake*, both of them are made of a Fish-shell, that they gather by the Sea side, *Wompompeag* is of the greater sort, and *Roanoake* of the lesser, and the *Wompompeag* is three times the value of *Roanoake* ; and these serue as Gold and Siluer doe heere ; they barter also one commoditie for another, and are very glad of trafficke and commerce, so farre as to supply their necessities : They shew no great desire of heaping wealth, yet some they will have to be buryed with them ; If they were Christians, and would live so free from covetousnesse, and many other vices which abound in Christendome, they would be a brave people.

I therefore conclude, that since God Almighty hath made this Countrey so large and fruit-full,

full, and that the people be such as you have heard them described; It is much more Prudence and Charity, to Civilize, and make them Chriſtians, then to kill, robbe, and hunt them from place to place, as you would doe a wolfe. By reducing of them, God ſhall be ſerued, his Majeſties Empire enlarged by the addition of many thouſand Subjects, as well as of large Territories, our Nation honoured, and the Planters themſelues enriched by the trafficke and commerce which may be had with them; and in many other things, they may be uſefull, but prejudiciall they cannot be, if it be not through their owne faults, by negligence of fortifying themſelues, and not conſeruing military diſcipline.

F   C H A P.

Chap. VI.

Conditions propounded by the Lord *Baltemore*, to such as shall goe, or adventure into *Mary-land*.

I.

HAT person soever, subject to our soveraigne Lord the King of *England*, shal be at the charge to transport into the Province of *Maryland*, himselfe or his deputy, with any number of able men, betweene the ages of 16 and 50, each man being provided in all things necessary for a Plantatiõ (which, together with their transportation, will amount to about 20 l. a man, as by an æstimate hereafter following may appeare) there shalbe assigned unto every such adventurer,

turer, for every five men which he shall so transport thither, a proportion of good land within the said Province, containing in quantity 1000 acres of English measure, which shall be erected into a Mannor, and be conveyed to him, his heires, and assignes for ever, with all such royalties and priviledges, as are usually belonging to Mannors in *England*; rendring and paying yerely unto his Lordship, and his heires for every such Mannor, a quit rent of 20 shillings, (to be paid in the Commodities of the Countrey) and such other services as shall be generally agreed upon for publike uses, and the common good.

II.

What person soever, as aforesaid, shall transport himselfe, or any lesse number of servants then five (aged, and provided as aforesaid) he shall have assigned to him, his heires and assignes for ever, for himselfe, 100 acres of good land within the said Province; and for and in respect of every such servant, 100 acres more, be be holden of his Lordship in freehold, paying therefore, a yeerely quit rent of 2 shillings for every hundred acres, in the Commodities of the Countrey.

III.

Any married man that shall transport him-

selfe

selfe, his wife and children; shall have assigned
unto him, his heires and assignes for ever, in free-
hold, (as aforesaid) for himselfe 100 acres; and
for his wife 100 acres; and for every child that
he shall carry over, under the age of 16 yeeres,
50 acres; paying for a quit rent 12 pence for
every fifty acres.

IIII.

Any woman that shall transport herselfe or
any children, under the age of sixe yeeres, shall
have the like Conditions as aforesaid.

V.

Any one that shall carry over any women
servants, under the age of fourty yeeres, shall
have for and in respect of every such woman
servant, 50 acres; paying onely a quit rent, as
aforesaid.

Instructions

Chap. VII.

Instructions and advertisements, for such as shall intend to goe, or send, to plant in Maryland.

His Countrey of *Maryland*, lieth from *England* to the Southwest, about 1200 leagues by Sea : the voyage is sometimes performed thither in 5 or 6 weekes, but ordinarily it is two moneths voyage, and oftner within that time then beyond it. The returne from thence to *England*, is ordinarily made in a moneth, and seldome exceeds sixe weekes.

The best time of the yeere for going thither, is to be there by *Michaelmas*, or at furthest by *Christmas*, for he that comes by that time shall have time enough to build him a house, and to prepare ground sufficient to plant in the spring following. But there is conveniency of passage thither in most moneths of the yeere; and any one that will send unto Mr. *Peasleys*, or Master *Morgans* house, may there be informed of the certaine time when any of his Lordships company is to goe away, and so save the charge of unnecessary attendance here in *London*.

A particular of such necessary provisions as every Adventurer must carry, according to the number of his servants : together with an estimate of their prices.

In Victualls.

For one man, for a yeere,

	l.	s	d
Imprimis, eight bushells of meale -	2	8	0
Item, two bushellls of Oatmeale	0	9	0
Item, one bushell of Pease	0	4	0
Item, one gallon of Oyle	0	3	6
Item, two gallons of Vinegar	0	2	0
Item, one gallon of Aquavitæ	0	2	6
Item, one bushell of Bay-salt	0	2	0
Item, in Sugar, Spice and Fruit	0	6	8
Summ.	3	17	8

In Apparrell.

For one man,

	l.	s	d
Item, two *Munmoth* caps or hats	0	4	0
Item, three falling Bands	0	1	3

Item,

Item, three shirts ——————— 0 —7 — 6
Item, one Waſtcoate ——————— 0 —2 — 2
Item, one ſuite of Canvas——— 0 —7 — 6
Item, one ſuite of Frize——————— 0 —10 — 0
Item, one ſuite of Cloth———— 0 — 16 — 0
Item, one courſe cloth, or frize coate 0 — 15 — 0
Item, three paire of ſtockings——— 0 —4 — 0
Item, ſixe paire of ſhooes ——— 0 — 13 — 0
Item, Inkle for garters——————— 0 — 0 — 2
Item, one dozen of points ——— 0 — 0 — 3
                    Summ.—— 4 ·— 0 — 10

In Bedding.

For two men.

	l	s	d
Item, two paire of Canvas ſheets	0	16	0
Item, ſeven ells of Canvas to make a bed and boulſter to be fill'd in the country	0	8	0
Item, one Rugg for a bed	0	8	0
Item, five ells of courſe Canvas to make a bed at Sea, to bee fill'd with ſtraw	0	4	0
Item, one courſe Rugg at Sea	0	6	0
Summ.	2	2	0
whereof one mans part is,	1	1	0

In

In Armes.

For one man,

	l	s	d
Item, one musket	1	0	0
Irem, 10 pound of Powder	0	11	0
Item, 40 pound of Lead, Bullets, Piſtoll and Gooſe ſhot, of each ſort ſome.	0	4	0
Item, one ſword,	0	5	0
Item, one belt	0	1	0
Item, one bandeleere and flaſke	0	2	0
Item, in Match	0	2	6
Summ.	2	5	6

In Tooles.

For five perſons , and ſo after the rate for more or leſſe.

	l	s	d
Item, 5 broad Howes, at 2 s. a piece	0	10	0
Item, 5 narrow Howes, at 16 d. a piece	0	6	8
Item, 2 broad Axes, at 3 s. 8 d. a piece	0	7	4
Item, 5 felling Axes, at 1 s. 6 d. a piece	0	7	6
Item, 2 ſteele Hand-ſawes, at 1 s. 4 d.	0	2	8
Item, 2 Two-handſawes at 5 s.	0	10	0
Item, a Whip-ſaw ſet and filed, with boxe, file and wreſt	0	10	0
Item, 2 Hammers, at 12 d.	0	2	0
Item, 3 Shovells, at 1 s. 6 d.	0	4	6

Item,

Item, 3 Spades, at 1 s. 6 d. ——————— 0 —— 4 —— 6
Item, 2 Awgurs, at 6 d. ——————— 0 —— 1 —— 0
Item, 6 Chissells, at 6 d. ——————— 0 —— 3 —— 0
Item, 2 Piercers stocked, at 4 d. ——— 0 —— 0 —— 8
Item, 3 Gimlets, at 2 d. ——————— 0 —— 0 —— 6
Item, 2 Hatchets, at 1 s. 9 d. ——— 0 —— 3 —— 6
Item, 2 Frowes to cleave Pales, at 1 s. 6 d. -- 0 —— 3 —— 0
Item, 2 Hand-bills, at 1 s. 8 d. ——— 0 —— 3 —— 4
Item, one Grindstone ——————— 0 —— 4 —— 0
Item, Nailes of all sorts ——————— 2 —— 0 —— 0
Item, 2 Pickaxes, at 1 s. 6 d. ——— 0 —— 3 —— 0

Summ. —— 6 —— 7 —— 2

whereof one mans part is —— 1 —— 5 —— 8

Houshold Implements.

For 6 persons, and so after the rate, for more

	l	s	d
Item, one Iron pot	0	7	0
Item, one Iron kettle	0	6	0
Item, one large Frying-pan	0	2	6
Item, one Gridiron	0	1	6
Item, two Skillets	0	5	0
Item, one Spit	0	2	0
Item, Platters, Dishes, and spoones of wood	0	4	0

Summ. —— 1 —— 8 —— 0

whereof one mans part is, —— 0 —— 4 —— 8

G   *An*

An estimate of the whole charge of transporting one seruant, and prouiding him of all necessaries for one yeere.

	l.	s.	d.
Inprimis, In Victualls	3	17	8
Item, In apparell	4	0	10
Item, In bedding	1	1	0
Item, In Armes	2	5	6
Item, In tooles	1	5	8
Item, In houshold Implements	0	4	8
Item, Caske to put his goods in	0	10	0
Item, fraight for his goods at halfe a tunne	1	10	0
Item, For his Victuall, and passage by Sea	6	0	0
	20.	15.	4

Of which charge, the Aduenturer hauing the greatest part of it in prouision & goods; in case any seruant die by the way, or shortly after his comming thither, the goods of that seruant being sold in the Countrey, will returne all his charge againe, with aduantage.

A Compu-

A Computation of a servants labour, and the profit that may arise by it, by instance in some particulars, which may be put in practise the first yeere.

l.———s.———d,

One man may at the season plant so much corne, as ordinarily yeelds of Wheate 100. bushels, worth upon the place, at Two shillings a Bushell. } ———10——— 0 —— 0

Of Beanes and Pease, 20. bushels, worth at three shillings a bushell. } ———3 ——— 0 —— 0

The same man will plant of *Tobacco*, betweene 800. and a 1000. weight, which at the lowest rate, at two pound 10. shil. the hundred, is worth, } ———20——— 0 —— 0

The same man may within the same yere, in the winter, make 4000. of Pipe-staves, worth upon the place foure pound the thousand. } ———16——— 0 —— 0

49.——————00——————00.

Beside all their other labours in building, fencing, clearing of ground, raising of Cattell, gardening, &c.

If

If a mans labour be imployed in Hempe and Flaxe, it will yeeld him as much profit, as *Tobacco* at this rate; and so in many other Commodities, whereof this Countrey is capable.

No man neede to doubt of the vent of these Commodities, for Merchants send shipping to those parts, who will buy off these Commodities at the aforesaid rates, in as great a quantitie, as they shalbe able to make ready for them; because they yeeld a great encrease of profit in other Countreys, which the Planters themselues may make aduantage of to themselues, if they have shipping, and thinke fit to deale in such a kind of trade. As for instance, a 1000. of Pipe-staves, which are rated upon the place at foure pound, being carried to the *Canaries*, will yeeld 15. or 20.l. Where likewise, and at the Westerne Islands, the *Indian* Corne will yeeld a great increase of benefit. The benefit also which may be raised by trade out of Swine onely, may easily be conceived to be very great, seeing they multiplie exceedingly, aske little tendance, and lesse charge of keeping in that Countrey, so abounding with Mast, Chestnuts, &c. For Porke being transported into *Spaine*, or the Westerne Ilands will yeeld about 6. pence a pound, and Bacon, 8.pence.or 9. pence.

A note

A note for the Aduenturers memory, of such things as hee may (if he please) carry with him , either for his owne better accommodation (on Ship-board, or for some time after his arrivall in Maryland) *or for trade, according to his abilitie.*

Provision for Ship-board.

FIne Wheate-flower, close and well packed, to make puddings , &c. Clarret-wine burnt. Canary Sacke. Conserues, Marmalades, Suckets, and Spices. Sallet Oyle. Prunes to stew. Live Poultry. Rice, Butter, Holland-cheese, or old Cheshire, gammons of Bacon , Porke, dried Neates-tongues, Beefe packed up in Vineger, some Weather-sheepe, meats baked in earthen potts, Leggs of Mutton minced, and stewed , and close packed up in tried Sewet, or Butter, in earthen pots: Iuyce of Limons, &c.

Provision for trade in *Virginia,* or *Maryland.*

If he be minded to furnish himselfe with
G 3   Cattell

Cattell in *Virginia*, his best way is to carry a superfluitie of wollen, or linnen cloth, callicoes, sayes, hatts, shooes, stockings, and all sorts of clothing; of Wine, Sugar, Prunes, Rasins, Currance, Honey, Spice, and Grocery wares, with which hee may procure himselfe cattell there, according to the stocke he dealeth withall. About 4. or 5. Pound laid out heere in commodities, will there buy a Cow; and betweene 20. and 30. shillings, a breeding Sow. The like Commodities will furnish him either there, or in *Maryland*, with Hogges, Poultry, and Corne. Hee may doe well also to carry a superfluity of Knives, Combes, and Bracelets, to trade with the women Natives; and some Hatchets, Howes, and Axes, to trade with the men for Venison, Fish, Turkies, Corne, Fawnes to store a Parke, &c.

Provision for his House.

Iron, and Locks, and Hinges, and bolts, &c. Mustard-seede, Glasse and Leade for his windowes, Mault for beere, a Hogshead of Beefe or Porke: Two or three Firkins of Butter, a hundred or two of old Cheeses; a gallon of honey, Soape and Candles, Iron wedges, Pookes for Rennet to make cheese: a good *Mastiffe*, &c.

Provision

Provision for Husbandry.

Seede Wheate, Rie, Barley, and Oates (the best way to preserue it from heating at sea, is to carry it in the eare) Kernells of Peares and Apples (especially of Pepins, Pearemaines, and Dufons) for the making hereafter of Cider, and Perry; the stones and seedes of all those fruits and rootes, and herbes, which he desireth to have. Good store of claver graffe seede, to make good meadow.

Provision for Fishing and Fowling.

Inprimis, necessaries for a boate of 3. or 4. Tunne; as Spikes, Nayles, Pitch, Tarre, Ocome, Canuis for a fayle, Ropes, Anchor, Iron for the Ruther: Fishing-lines for Cod and Macrills, &c. Cod-hookes, and Macrill-hookes, a Seane or Bafse-net, Herring-netts, Leade, Fowling-pieces of fixe foote; Powder and Shott, and Flint Stones; a good Water-Spaniell, &c.

A direct-

A direction for choice of feruants.

IN the taking of servants, he may doe well to furnifh himfelfe with as many as he can, of ufefull and neceffary Arts: A Carpenter, of all others the moft neceffary; A Mill-wright, Ship-wright, Boate-wright, Wheele-wright, Brick-maker, Brick-layer, Potter; one that can cleave Lath and Pale, and make Pipe-ftaves, &c. A Ioyner, Cooper, Turner, Sawyer, Smith, Cutler, Leather-dreffer, Miller, Fifherman, and Gardiner. Thefe will be of moft ufe; but any lufty young able man, that is willing to labour and take paines, although he have no particular trade, will be beneficiall enough to his Mafter.

And in cafe any Adventurer fhall be unprovided of fuch men to fupply his number, hee may have directions at the place where thefe bookes are to bee had, how and where hee may provide himfelfe of as many as hee pleafe.

The

The forme of binding a servant.

This Indenture *made the*   *day of*
       in the
yeere of our Soveraigne Lord King Charles, *&c.*
betweene   *of the one*
party, and   *on the*
other party, Witnesseth, *that the said*
       doth hereby covenant promise, and
grant, to and with the said
his Executors and Assignes, to serve him from
the day of the date hereof, vntill his first and
next arrivall in Maryland; *and after for and*
during the tearme of   *yeeres, in such*
service and imployment, as he the said
       or his assignes shall there im-
ploy him, according to the custome of the Countrey
in the like kind. In consideration whereof, the said
       doth promise
and grant, to and with the said
       to pay for his passing, and to
find him with Meat, Drinke, Apparell and Lodg-
ing, with other necessaries during the said terme;
and at the end of the said terme, to give him one
whole yeeres provision of Corne, and fifty acres of
Land, according to the order of the countrey. In
witnesse whereof, the said
hath hereunto put his hand and seale, the day and
yeere above written.

    Sealed and delivered in
       the presence of   H   The

The vsuall terme of binding a seruant, is for
five yeers; but for any artificer, or one that shall
deserue more then ordinary, the Aduenturer
shall doe well to shorten that time, and adde
encouragements of another nature (as he shall
see cause) rather then to want such vsefull men.

A Forme of a Bill of Lading, to be taken from
the Master of the Sip, by every Aduenterer,
for the better securing of the transportation of his goods.

*Shipped by the grace of God in goood order, and
well conditioned by*

                                    *in and
upon the good Ship, called the*
                              *whereof is master, vn-
der God, for this present voyage*
                              *and now riding at anker in the
                              and by Gods grace,*
bound for   *to say
being marked and numbred, as in the margent, and
are to be delivered in the like good order and well
conditioned, at the Port of Saint* Maries, *in* Maryland (*the danger of the Seas onely excepted*) *vn-
to*   *or to
assignes,*   *paying fraught for
                                          the*

the said goods
with primage and avarage accustomed. In wit-
nesse whereof, the Master or Purser of the said ship
hath affirmed to three Bills of Lading, all of this
tenor and date, the one of which three bills being
accomplished, the other two to stand void. And so
God send the good Ship to her desired Port in safe-
ty. Amen. Dated in

There is order taken for convenient houses
to be set up at Saint *Maries*, where all strangers
may at their first comming bee entertained,
with lodging and other fitting accommodations, for themselves and their goods, till they
can better provide for themselves.

The

The names of the Gentlemen adventurers that
are gone in perfon to this Plantation.

Mr. {
Leonard Calvert, the governor } his Lordfhips brothers.
George Calvert.
Ierome Hawley.   Efq; } Commiffioners.
Thomas Cornewallis. Efq;

(Baronet.

Richard Gerard, fon to Sir *Thomas Gerard* Knight and
Edward Wintour. } fonnes of the Lady *Anne Wintour*.
Freder: Wintour.
Henry Wifeman, fon to Sir *Thomas Wifeman* Knight.
Iohn Saunders.
Edward Cranfield.
Henry Greene.
Nicholas Ferfax.
Iohn Baxter.
Thomas Dorrell.
Captaine *Iohn Hill*.
Iohn Medcalfe.
William Saire.

THE CHARTER
OF
MARY LAND.

HARLES By the
Grace of GOD, King of
England, Scotland, France,
and *Ireland,* Defendor
of the Faith, &c. To all
to whom thefe Prefents
fhall come greeting.

WHEREAS Our right Trufty and
Wellbeloved Subject *Cecilius Caluert,* Baron
of *Baltemore* in our Kingdom of *Ireland,* Sonne
and heire of Sir *George Caluert* Knight, late Ba-

A 2   ron

ron of *Baltemore* in the same Kingdome of *Ireland*, pursuing his Fathers intentions, being excited with a laudable and pious zeale for the propagation of the Christian Faith, and the enlargement of our Empire and Dominion, hath humbly besought leave of Vs, by his industry and charge, to transport an ample Colony of the *English* Nation unto a certaine Countrey hereafter described, in the parts of *America*, not yet cultivated and planted, though in some parts thereof inhabited by certaine barbarous people, having no knowledge of Almighty God, and hath humbly besought our Royall Majestie to give, grant, and confirme all the said Countrey, with certaine Priviledges and Iurisdictions, requisite for the good government, and state of his Colony, and Countrey aforesaid, to him and his heires for ever.

The bounds.   KNOW YEE therefore, that Wee favouring the Pious, and Noble purpose of the said Barons of *Baltemore*, of our speciall grace, certaine knowledge, and meere motion, have given, granted, and confirmed, and by this our present Charter, for Vs, Our Heires, and Successors, doe give, grant and confirme unto the said *Cecilius*, now Baron of *Baltemore*, his heires and Assignes, all that part of a *Peninsula*, lying in the parts of *America*, betweene the Ocean on the East, and the Bay of *Chesopeack* on the West, and divided from the other part thereof, by by a right line drawne from the Promontory or Cape of Land called *Watkins Point* (situate in the foresaid Bay, neere the river of *Wighco*) on the West, unto the maine Ocean on the East; and betweene that bound on the South, unto that part of *Delaware* Bay on the North, which lieth under the fortieth degree of Northerly Latitude from the Equinoctiall, where *New-England* ends; And all that tract of land betweene the bounds aforesaid; that is to say, passing from the foresaid Bay, called *Delaware* Bay, in a right line by the degree aforesaid, unto the true Meridian of the first fountaine of the River of *Pattowmeck*, and from thence trending toward the South unto the farther banke of the fore-said River, and following the West and South side thereof unto a certaine place called *Cinquack*, situate neere the mouth of the said River, where it falls into the Bay of *Chesopeack*, and from thence by a straight line unto the foresaid Promontory, and place called *Watkins Point*, (So that all that tract of land divided by the line aforesaid, drawne betweene the maine Ocean, and *Watkins Point* unto the Promontory called *Cape Charles*, and all its apurtenances, doe remaine intirely excepted to us, our heires, and Successors for ever.)

WEE DOE also grant and confirme unto the said now Lord *Baltemore*, his heires and Assignes, all Ilands, and Iletts within the

limits

limitts aforesaid, and all and singular the Ilands and Iletts, which are, or shall be in the Ocean, within 10. Leagues from the Easterne shoare of the said Countrey, towards the East, with all and singular Ports, Harbors, Bayes, Rivers, and Inletts, belonging unto the Countrey, or Ilands aforesaid: And all the Soile, lands, Fields, Woods, Mountaines, Fennes, Lakes, Rivers, Bayes, and Inletts, situate, or being within the bounds, and limits aforesaid, with the fishing of all sorts of fish, *whales, Sturgeons,* and all other royal fishes in the Sea, Bays, Inletts, or Rivers, within the premises: and the fish therein taken: and moreover all Veines, Mines, and Quarries, aswell discovered, as not discovered, of Gold, Siluer, Gemmes, and pretious stones, and all other whatsoever, be it of Stones, Mettalls, or of any other thing, or matter whatsoever, found, or to bee found within the Countrey, Iles, and limits aforesaid. And Furthermore the Patronages and Aduowsons of all Churches, which (as Christian Religion shall encrease within the Countrey, Iles, Iletts, and limits aforesaid) shall happen hereafter to bee erected: together with licence and power, to build and found Churches, Chappells, and Oratories, in convenient and fit places within the premises, and to cause them to be dedicated, and consecrated according to the Ecclesiasticall Lawes
of

of our Kingdome of *England* : *Together with* all
and singular the like, and as ample rights, Iurisdictions, Priviledges, Prerogatives, Royalties,
Liberties Immunities, Royall rights, and franchises of what kind soever temporall, as well by
Sea, as by land, within the Countrey, Iles, Iletts, and limits aforesaid; To have, exercise, *Iurisdiction*
use and enjoy the same, as amply as any Bishop *of a Count*
of *Durham*, within the Bishoprick, or County Palatine.
Palatine of *Durham*, in our Kingdome of *England*, hath at any time heretofore had, held, used, or enjoyed, or of right ought, or might have
had, held, used, or enjoyed.

AND HIM the said now Lord *Baltemore*, his Heires and Assignes, Wee doe by
these Presents for Vs, Our Heires and Successors, make, create, and constitute the true and
absolute Lords, and Proprietaries of the Countrey aforesaid, and of all other the Premises,
(except before excepted) saving alwayes, the
faith and allegeance, and Soveraigne dominion due unto Vs, Our Heires and Successors.

TO HAVE, hold, possesse, and enjoy the
sayd Countrey, Iles, Iletts, and other the Premises, unto the said now Lord *Baltemore*,
his heires and assignes, to the sole and proper
use and behoofe of him the said now Lord
Baltemore, his heires and assignes for ever.

TO BEE holden of Vs, Our Heires, and *Tenure.*
Successors, Kings of *England*, as of Our Castle
of

of *Windfor*, in Our County of *Berkſhire*, in free
and common foccage, by fealty onely, for all
feruices, and not in Capite, or by Knights fer-
uice : YEELDING and paying therefore
to Vs, our Heires and Succeſſors, two *Indian*
Arrowes of thoſe parts, to be delivered at Our
faid Caſtle of *Windfor*, every yeere on the Tuef-
day in *Eaſter* weeke; and alfo the fifth part of
all Gold and Siluer Oare within the limits
aforefaid, which ſhall from time to time happen to be found.

Rent.

NOW THAT the faid Countrey thus
by Vs granted, and defcribed, may be eminent
above all other parts of the faid territory, and
dignified with larger titles : Know yee that wee
of our further grace, certaine knowledge, and
meere motion, have thought fit to erect the
fame Countrey and Ilands into a Province, as
out of the fullneſſe of Our royall Power, and
Prerogative, Wee doe, for Vs, Our Heires, and
Succeſſors, erect, and incorporate them into a
Province, and doe call it *Mary land*, and fo
from henceforth will have it called.

AND FORASMVCH as Wee
have hereby made, and ordained the forefaid
now Lord *Baltemore*, the true Lord, and
Proprietary of all the Province aforefaid :
Know yee therefore moreover, that Wee,
repofing efpeciall truft and confidence in
the fidelitie, wifedome, Iuftice, and Provi-
dent

dent circumspection of the said now Lord Baltemore, for Vs, Our Heires and Succeſſors, doe grant free, full, and abſolute power, by vertue of theſe Preſents, to him and his heires, for the good and happy government of the ſaid Province, to ordaine, make, enact, and under his and their ſeales to publiſh any Lawes whatſoever, appertaining either unto the publike State of the ſaid Province, or unto the private utility of particular Perſons, according unto their beſt diſcretions, of and with the aduiſe aſſent and approbation of the Free-men of the ſaid Province, or the greater part of them, or of their delegates or deputies, whom for the enacting of the ſaid Lawes, when, and as often as neede ſhall require, We will that the ſaid now Lord Baltemore, and his heires, ſhall aſſemble in ſuch ſort and forme, as to him or them ſhall ſeeme beſt: And the ſame lawes duly to execute upon all people, within the ſaid Province, and limits thereof, for the time being, or that ſhall be conſtituted under the government, and power of him or them, either ſayling towards Mary-land, or returning from thence toward England, or any other of Ours, or forraine Dominions, by impoſition of Penalties, Impriſonment, or any other puniſhment; yea, if it ſhall be needfull, and that the quality of the offence require it, by taking away member or life, either by him the ſaid now Lord

B   Baltemore,

Baltemore,and his heires, or by his or their Deputies, Lievtenants , Iudges , Iustices , Magistrates, Officers, and Ministers to be ordained or appointed, according to the Tenor, and true intention of thefe Prefents : And likewife to appoint and eftablifh any Iudges and Iustices, Magistrates and Officers whatfoever, at fea and Land, for what caufes foever , and with what power foever , and in fuch forme, as to the faid now Lord *Baltemore* , or his heires , fhall feeme moft conuenient: Alfo to remit, releafe, pardon, and abolifh , whether before Iudgement, or after , all crimes or offences whatfoever, againft the faid Lawes : and to doe all and every other thing or things, which unto the compleate eftablifhment of Iuftice , unto Courts, Prætories, and Tribunals, formes of Iudicature and maners of proceeding, do belong: although in thefe Prefents, expreffe mention be not made thereof, and by Iudges by them delegated, to award Proceffe, hold Pleas, and determine in all the faid Courts and Tribunalls , all actions, fuits, and caufes whatfoever, as well criminall as civill, perfonall, reall, mixt, and prætoriall; which laws, fo as aforfaid to be publifhed, Our pleafure is, and fo Wee enioyne, require, and command, fhall be moft abfolute and avaiable in Law , and that all the Leige people, and fubjects of Vs , Our Heires and Succeffors, do obferue and keepe the fame inuiolably,

in

in those parts, so farre as they concerne them, under the paines therein expressed, or to be expressed: Provided neverthelesse, that the said Lawes be consonant to reason, and be not repugnant or contrary, but as neere as conveniently may be, agreeable to the Lawes, Statutes, Customes, and Rights of this our Kingdome of *England*.

AND FORASMVCH, as in the Government of so great a Province, suddaine accidents doe often happen, whereunto it will be necessary to apply a remedy, before the Free-holders of the said Province, their Delegates, or Deputies, can be assembled to the making of Lawes, neither will it be convenient, that instantly upon every such emergent occasion, so great a multitude should be called together: Therefore for the better government of the said Province, Wee will and ordaine, and by these Presents for Vs, Our Heires, and Successors, doe grant unto the said now Lord *Baltemore*, and his heires, that the said now Lord *Baltemore* and his heires, by themselues, or by their Magistrates and Officers in that behalfe duely to be ordained as aforesaid, may make and constitute, fit and wholesome Ordinances, from time to time, within the said Province, to be kept and obserued, as well for the preservation of the Peace, as for the better government of the people there inhabiting, and publikely

to

to notifie the same to all persons, whom the same doth, or any way may concerne; which Ordinances, Our pleasure is, shall be observed inviolably within the said Province, under the paines therein to bee expressed. So as the said Ordinances be consonant to reason, and be not repugnant nor contrary, but so farre as conveniently may be, agreeable with the Lawes and Statutes of Our Kingdome of *England*, and so as the said Ordinances be not extended, in any sort to bind, charge, or take away the right or interest of any person, or persons, of, or in their Life, Member, Free-hold, Goods, or Chattells.

Licence to goe to Mary land. FVRTHERMORE, that this new Colony may the more happily encrease by the multitude of people resorting thither, and may likewise be the more strongly defended from the incursions of Saluages, or other enemies, Pyrates and Robbers: Therefore Wee, for Vs, Our Heires and Successors, doe give and grant by those Presents, Power, licence, and liberty unto all the liege people, and subjects, both present, and future, of Vs, Our Heires, and Successors (excepting those who shall be specially forbidden) to transport themselues and families unto the said Province, with conuenient shipping, and fitting provisions, and there to settle themselues, dwell and inhabite, and to build, and fortifie Castles, Forts, and other places of strength,

strength for the publike, and their owne private defence, at the appointment of the said now Lord *Baltemore*, and his heires, the Statute of fugitives, or any other whatsoever, to the contrary of the premises, in any wise notwithstanding.

AND WEE will also, and of Our more *People borne* speciall grace, for Vs, Our Heires, and Succes- *in* Mary- sors, wee doe straightly enioyne, constitute, land, *made* ordaine, and command, that the said Province *Denizens of* shall be of Our Allegiance, and that all and sin- England. gular the Subjects, and Liege people of Vs, Our Heires, and Successors, transported, or to be transported into the said Province, and the children of them, and of such as shall descend from them, there already borne, or hereafter to be borne, bee, and shall be Denizens, and Lieges of Vs, Our Heires, and Successors, of Our Kingdome of *England*, and *Ireland*, and be in all things held, treated, reputed, and esteemed as the liege faithfull people of Vs, Our Heires, and Successors, borne within Our Kingdome of *England*: and likewise any Lands, Tenements, Revenues, Seruices, and other hereditaments whatsoever, within Our Kingdome of *England*, and other Our Dominions, may inherite, or otherwise purchase, receive, take, have, hold, buy, and possesse, and them may occupy, and enjoy, give, sell, aliene, and bequeath, as likewise, all Liberties, Franchises, and Priviledges, of this

Our

Our Kingdome of *England*, freely, quietly, and peaceably, have and possesse, occupy and enjoy, as Our liege people, borne, or to be borne, within Our said Kingdome of *England*, without the let, molestation, vexation, trouble, or grievance of Vs, Our Heires and Successors: any Statute, Act, Ordinance, or Provision to the contrary hereof notwithstanding.

Licence to transport goods and merchandise AND FVRTHERMORE, That Our Subjects may be the rather encouraged to undertake this expedition, with ready and cheerefull minds; KNOW YEE, that We of Our speciall grace, certaine knowledge, and meere motion, doe give and grant, by vertue of these presents, aswell unto the said now Lord *Baltemore* and his Heires, as to all other that shall from time to time repaire unto that province, with a purpose to inhabite there, or to trade with the Natives of the said Province, full licence to Lade and Fraight in any Ports whatsoever, of Vs, Our Heires and Successors, and into the said Province of *Maryland*, by them, their servants, or assignes, to transport, all and singular, their Goods, Wares, and Merchandize; as likewise all sorts of graine whatsoever, and any other things whatsoever, necessary for food or clothing (not prohibited by the Lawes and Statutes of our Kingdomes and Dominions to bee carried out of the said kingdomes) without any lett, or molestation of

Vs,

Vs, Our Heires, or Succeſſors, or of any of the officers of Vs, Our Heires, or Succeſſors; (ſaving alwayes, to Vs, Our Heires and Succeſſors, the Impoſitions, Cuſtomes, and other duties and payments for the ſaid Wares and Merchandiſe) any Statute, Act, Ordinance or other thing whatſoever to the contrary notwithſtanding.

AND becauſe in ſo remote a Country, and ſituate amongſt ſo many barbarous nations, the incurſions aſwell of the ſalvages themſelves, as of other enemies, pyrates and robbers, may probably be feared : Therefore We have given, and for Vs, Our Heires, and Succeſſors, doe give power by theſe preſents, unto the now Lord *Baltemore*, his heires and aſſignes, by themſelves, or their Captaines, or other their officers, to Leauy, Muſter and Traine, all ſorts of men, of what condition, or whereſoever borne, in the ſaid Province of *Mary-land* for the time being, and to make warre, and to purſue the Enemies and Robbers aforeſaid, aſwell by ſea as by land, yea, even without the limits of the ſaid Province, and (by Gods aſſiſtance) to vanquiſh and take them, and being taken, to put them to death by the Law of warre, or to ſave them at their pleaſure, and to doe all and every other thing which unto the charge and office of a Captaine Generall of an Army belongeth, or hath accuſtomed to belong, as fully and freely,

Power of warr and peace.

as any Captaine Generall of an army hath ever had the same.

A L S O, Our Will and Pleasure is, and by this Our Charter, We doe give unto the said now Lord *Baltemore*, his heires, and assignes, full power, liberty, and authority, in case of Rebellion, Tumult, or Sedition, if any should happen (which God forbid) either upon the land within the Province aforesaid, or upon the maine sea, in making a voyage thither, or returning from thence, by themselues, or their captains, deputies or other officers, to be authorized under their seales for that purpose (to whom we also, for Vs, Our Heires and Successors, doe give and grant by these presents, full power and authority) to exercise Martiall Law against mutinous and seditious persons of those parts, such as shall refuse to submit themselves to his, or their governement, or shall refuse to serve in the warres, or shall flie to the Enemy, or forsake their Ensignes, or be loyterers, or straglers, or otherwise howsoever offending against the Law, Custome, and Discipline military, as freely, and in as ample manner and forme, as any Captaine generall of an army by vertue of his office might, or hath accustomed to use the same.

F V R T H E R M O R E, That the way to honors and dignities, may not seeme to be altogether precluded and shut up, to men well

borne,

borne, and such as shall prepare themselves unto this present Plantation, and shall desire to deserve well of Vs, and Our Kingdomes, both in peace and war, in so farre distant and remote a Countrey: Therefore We, for Vs, Our Heires and Succeessors, doe give free, and absolute power, unto the said now Lord *Baltemore*, his heires and assignes, to conferre favours, rewards, and honours, upon such inhabitants within the Province aforesaid, as shall deserve the same; and to invest them, with what titles and dignities soever, as he shall thinke fit, (so as they be not such as are now used in *England*) As likewise to erect and incorporate, Townes into Boroughes, and Boroughs into Cities, with convenient priuiledges and immunities, according to the merit of the inhabitants, and the fitnesse of the places, and to doe all and every other thing or things, touching the premises, which to him, or them, shall seeme meete and requisite; albeit they be such as of their owne nature might otherwise require a more speciall commandement and warrant, then in these Presents is expressed.

W E E will also, and by these Presents, for Vs, Our Heires and Succeessors, We doe give and grant licence, by this Our Charter, unto the said now Lord *Baltemore*, his heires and assignes, and to all the inhabitants and dwellers in the Province aforesaid, both present and to come,

come, to import, or unlade, by themselves, or their servants factors, or assignes, all Merchandizes and goods whatsoever, that shall arise of the fruits and commodities of the said Province, either by land or sea, into any of the ports of Vs, Our Heires and Successors, in Our kingdomes of *England*, or *Ireland*, or otherwise to dispose of the said goods, in the said Ports, and if need be, within one yeere next after the unlading of the same, to lade the said merchandizes and goods againe, into the same or other ships, and to export the same into any other Countreys, either of our Dominion or forreigne, (being in Amity with Vs, Our Heires and Successors) Provided alwayes, that they pay such Customes, Impositions, Subsidies and Duties for the same, to Vs, Our Heires and Successors, as the rest of Our Subjects of Our Kingdome of *England*, for the time being, shall be bound to pay: beyond which, We will not that the inhabitants of the foresaid Province of *Mary-land*, shall be any way charged.

AND furthermore, of Our more ample and speciall Grace, certaine knowledge, and meere motion, We doe, for Vs, Our Heires and Successors, grant unto the said now Lord *Baltemore*, his heires and assignes, full and absolute power and authority, to make, erect, and constitute, within the Province of *Mary-land*, and the Iles and Iletts aforesaid, such, and so many Seaports,

ports, Harbours, Creekes, and other places, for discharge and unlading of goods and merchandises, out of Ships, Boates, and other vessells, and lading them, and in such and so many places, and with such Rights, Iurisdictions, Liberties and Priviledges unto the said ports belonging, as to him or them shall seeme most expedient. And that all and singular the Ships, Boats, and other Vessells, which shall come for merchandize and trade unto the said Province, or out of the same shall depart; shall be laden and unladen only at such Ports as shall be so erected and constituted by the said now Lord *Baltemore*, his heires or assignes, any Vse, Custome, or other thing to the contrary notwithstanding; saving alwayes unto Vs, Our heires and Successors, and to all the Subjects (of Our Kingdome of *England* and *Ireland*) of Vs, Our Heires and Successors, free liberty of fishing for Sea-fish, aswell in the Sea, Bayes, Inletts, and navigable Rivers, as in the Harbours, Bayes and Creekes of the Province aforesaid, and the Priviledges of salting and drying their fish on the shore of the said Province; and for the same cause, to cut and take underwood, or twiggs there growing, and to build Cottages and Shedds necessary in this behalfe, as they heretofore have, or might reasonably have used; which Liberties and Priviledges, neverthelesse, the Subjects aforesaid, of Vs, Our Heires and

Succes-

Succeſſors, ſhall enjoy without any notable dammage, or injury, to be done to the ſaid now Lord *Baltemore*, his heires, or aſſignes, or to the dwellers and inhabitants of the ſaid Province, in the Ports, Creekes and ſhores aforeſaid, and eſpecially in the woods and Copſes growing within the ſaid Province: And if any ſhall doe any ſuch dammage, or injury, he ſhall incurre the heavy diſpleaſure of Vs, Our Heires and Succeſſors, the puniſhment of the Lawes, and ſhall moreover make ſatisfaction.

WEE doe furthermore, will, appoint, and ordaine, and by theſe Preſents, for Vs, Our Heires and Succeſſors, We doe grant unto the ſaid now Lord *Baltemore*, his heires and aſſignes, that he the ſaid Lord *Baltemore*, his heires and aſſignes, may from time to time for ever, have and enjoy, the Cuſtomes and Subſidies, in the Ports, Harbours, and other Creekes and places aforeſaid, within the Province aforeſaid; payable, or due for merchandizes and wares, there to be laded or unladed, the ſaid Cuſtomes and Subſidies to be reaſonably aſſeſſed (upon any occaſion) by themſelves and the people there, as aforeſaid; to whom we give power by theſe Preſents, for Vs, Our Heires and Succeſſors upon juſt cauſe, and in a due proportion, to aſſeſſe and impoſe the ſame.

Power to cre-
ate Tenures.

AND FVRTHER, of Our ſpeciall grace, and of Our certaine knowledge, and
meere

meere motion, Wee have given granted, and confirmed, and by thefe Ptefents for Vs, Our Heires and Succeffors, doe give, grant, and confirme unto the faid now Lord *Baltemore*, his heires and affignes, full and abfolute licence, power, and authoritie, that hee the faid now Lord *Baltemore*, his heires and affignes, from time to time hereafter for ever, at his, or their will, and pleafure, may affigne, aliene, grant, demife, or enfeoffe of the Premifes fo many, and fuch parts and parcells, to him or them that fhall be willing to purchafe the fame, as they fhall thinke fit, TO HAVE and to hold to them the fayd perfon, or perfons, willing to take or purchafe the fame, their heires and affignes in fee fimple, or fee taile, or for terme of life, or lives, or yeeres, to bee held of the faid now Lord *Baltemore*, his heires, and affignes, by fuch feruices, cuftomes, and rents, as fhall feeme fit to the faid now Lord *Baltemore*, his heires and affignes; and not immediately of Vs, Our Heires or Succeffors: and to the fame perfon or perfons, and to all and every of them. Wee doe give and grant by thefe Prefents for Vs, Our Heires and Succeffors, licence, authoritie, and power, that fuch perfon or perfons may take the premifes, or any parcell thereof, of the forefaid now Lord *Baltemore*, his heires or affignes, and the fame hold to themfelues, their heires, or affignes, (in what

C 3   eftate

eſtate of inheritance ſoever, in fee ſimple, or in fee taile, or otherwiſe, as to them, and the now Lord *Baltemore*, his heires and aſſignes, ſhall ſeeme expedient) of the ſaid now Lord *Baltemore*, his heires and aſſignes; the ſtatute made in the Parliament of *Edward*, Sonne of King *Henry*, late King of *England*, Our Predeceſſor, commonly called the Statute *Quia emptores terrarum*, lately publiſhed in Our Kingdome of *England*, or any other Statute, Acte, Ordinance, Vſe, Law, or Cuſtome, or any other thing, cauſe, or matter thereupon heretofore had, done, publiſhed, ordained, or provided to the contrary, in any wiſe notwithſtanding; And by theſe Preſents, Wee give, and grant licence unto the ſaid now Lord *Baltemore*, and his heires, to erect any parcells of land within the Province aforeſaid, into Mannors, and in every of the ſaid Mannors, to have, and to hold a *Court Baron*, with all things whatſoever, which to a *Court Baron* doe belong, and to have and hold viewe of *Franck-pledge*, (for the conſeruation of the peace, and the better government of thoſe Parts,) by themſelues or their ſtewards, or by the Lords for the time being of other Mannors, to bee deputed, when they ſhall bee erected : and in the ſame, to uſe all things belonging to *View of Franck-Pledge*.

AND FVRTHER, Our pleaſure is, and by theſe

thefe Prefents, for Vs, Our Heires, and Succeffors, wee doe covenant and grant to and with
the faid now Lord *Baltemore*, his heires and affignes; That Wee, Our Heires and Succeffors,
fhall at no time hereafter, fet, or make, or caufe
to be fet, any Impofition, Cuftome, or other
Taxation, Rate, or Contribution whatfoever,
in or upon the dwellers and inhabitants of the
forefaid Province, for their Lands, Tenements,
goods or Chattells within the faid Province, or
in or upon any goods or merchandizes, within
the faid Province, or to be laden, or unladen
within any the Ports or harbours of the faid
Province : And Our pleafure is, and for Vs,
Our Heires, and Succeffors, Wee charge and
command, that this Our Declaration fhall be
henceforward from time to time received, and
allowed in all Our Courts, and before all the
Iudges of Vs Our Heires and Succeffors, for a
fufficient and lawfull difcharge, payment, and
acquittance; Commanding all and fingular,
our Officers and Minifters of Vs, our Heires
and Succeffors, and enjoyning them upon paine
of Our high difpleafure, that they doe not pre-
fume at any time to attempt any thing to the
contrary of the premifes, or that they doe in
any fort withftand the fame, but that they be
at all times ayding and affifting, as is fitting,
unto the faid now Lord *Baltemore*, and his
heires, and to the Inhabitants, and Merchants
of

of *Maryland* aforesaid, their seruants, ministers, factors and assignes, in the full use and fruition of the benefit of this Our Charter.

AND FVRTHER, Our pleasure is, and by these Presents for Vs , our heires and Successors, VVee doe grant unto the said now Lord *Baltemore*, his heires and assignes , and to the Tenants, and Inhabitants of the said Province of *Mary-land*, both present, and to come, and to every of them, that the said Province, Tenants , and Inhabitants of the said *Colony* or Countrey , shall not from henceforth bee held or reputed as a member , or' a part of the land of *Virginia*, or of any other Colony whatsoever, now transported, or hereafter to be transported, nor shall be depending on , or subject to their government in any thing, from whom VVee doe separate that, and them, and Our pleasure is, by these Presents that they bee separated, and that they be subject immediately to Our Crowne of *England*, as depending thereof for ever.

AND IF PERCHANCE hereafter it should happen, that any doubts or questions should arise, concerning the true sence and understanding of any word, clause, or sentece contained in this Our present Charter , Wee will, ordaine, and command, that at all times, and in all things, such Interpretation bee made thereof, and allowed in any of Our Courts whatsoever,

ver, as fhall be judged moft aduantagious, and favourable unto the the faid now Lord *Balte-more*, his heires and affignes. PROVIDED alwayes, that no Interpretation bee admitted thereof, by which Gods Holy and Truely Chriftian Religion, or the allegeance due unto Vs, Our Heires and Succeffors, may in any thing fuffer any prejudice, or diminution.

ALTHOVGH expreffe mention bee not made in thefe Prefents, of the true yeerely value, or certainty of the premifes, or of any part thereof, or of other gifts and grants, made by Vs, Our Heires, and Predeceffors, unto the faid now Lord *Baltemore*, or any Statute, Acte, Ordinance, Provifion, Proclamation, or reftraint heretofore had, made, publifhed, ordained, or provided, or any other thing, caufe, or matter whatfoever to the contrary thereof in any wife notwithftanding.

IN WITNESSE whereof, Wee have caufed thefe Our Letters to bee made Pattents. Witneffe Our felfe at *weftminfter*, the Twentieth day of *Iune*, In the Eighth yeere of Our Reigne.

D

DATE DUE

GAYLORD   PRINTED IN U.S.A.